YOUTUBE: THE 2018 ESSENTIAL GUIDE TO GROW YOUR YOUTUBE CHANNEL AND MAKE MONEY FAST

TABLE OF CONTENTS

INTRODUCTION

Growing a YouTube channel and more importantly making money from it is a growing problem for most people who intend to start a YouTube channel. I think that, in 2018, people are of the opinion that it's somehow more difficult to start a YouTube channel because of the amount of competition and saturation in the YouTube market. I want to emphasize that this is a new guide, so all of the information is cutting edge and current. Some people don't even know of these techniques yet as they're so recent.

Whether you're a kid, teenager or an adult, the aim of this book is to tell you exactly how, step by step, it is possible to not only start a successful YouTube channel, but that right now is the best time ever to become successful FAST. If you apply the contents of this guide, within a few months you'll be well on your way to tens of thousands of subscribers and possibly thousands of dollars a month in earnings. No matter which country you're from, this guide will work for you!

In this short guide, you're going to learn exactly how to build your YouTube channel from the ground up and the exact way that huge YouTuber's like Pewdiepie, Jake Paul, Jenna Marbles, h3h3 and many others got so big and exactly how you can too. This guide will also discuss the main sources of income from YouTube and how you can maximally monetize your YouTube channel. We'll delve deeply into the pros and cons of monetization strategies and the different ways to promote your YouTube channel.

Specifically, you'll learn...

- How to make a YouTube channel in 2018
- Techniques for top quality content on YouTube.
- The exact way to pick a niche to make content on to make content you're passionate about.
- The secrets to program your YouTube channel for EXPLOSIVE growth
- A step by step guide on collaborating with other YouTubers to promote your channel.
- The best 2018 Vlogging equipment on the market for any budget
- The current equipment you might need to start making a Gaming Channel.
- Exactly how to get noticed on YouTube.
- How YouTubers make massive money and how you can too
- How you can use YouTube to make more money than you can dream of

So, without further introduction, let's jump in with a discussion of "how to make a YouTube channel"...

CHAPTER 1

HOW TO MAKE A YOUTUBE CHANNEL

Regardless of your purpose for creating a YouTube channel, it doesn't take time to create one. After your channel has been created and approved, you can change its appearance, edit your videos if necessary and perhaps group your videos into different playlists. Whether you are creating your YouTube account for your business or brand, here is a simple 3-step checklist you can follow;

1. Create A Google Account

This is important provided you didn't have one previously. By default, your YouTube username will be your google username. Hence, when you upload your videos, this username is what everyone else sees. However, you are free to change it once you're on YouTube. If you have a Gmail account, you have a Google account and you have access to all Google products such as Google play, Google drive, and YouTube.

But before you can sign onto YouTube from your Google account, you will be asked to provide your first and last name. This is the name that will be used to identify you on YouTube. Hence, you can either choose between a different name or choose your actual first and last name.

Choose Your Character:

The name of your YouTube channel, as you know, is very important. I would say the popular YouTubers are split almost equally between using their real name and a brand name. Now, this really depends on your preference for privacy and what your channel content is going to be about. For example, most vlogging channels tends to use their full name, whereas most gaming channels tend to use a brand or made up name. Be creative.

If your channel is going to be about an idea, concept or a brand channel then you're going to want to use the brand name. Coming up with a brand name is something you should think about long and hard. A few tips that you can mix and match:

- Alliteration e.g. "Charisma on Command"
- Wordplay/Rhyming e.g. "Pewdiepie"
- Try a single word e.g. "Vsauce", "Smosh"

That being said, your channel name isn't overly important as long as the content is quality. For example, most cannot even pronounce the channel name "Kurzgesagt", however their videos consistently pull millions of views. Pick a name you like and are passionate about, and stick with it.

Once you have filled these required fields, select "Create Channel".

2. Customize the appearance of your channel

This is important since the first impression of your channel is extremely important. Of course, the quality of your videos is supreme above all the rest, however the truth it's best to cover all your bases.

Some of the basic things you can change are your;

- Channel's icon
- Channel's art
- Channel's description.

When you want to make these changes, go to your channel, and click the edit button next to the items you want to change.

Channel Icon

This can be an interesting photo of yourself, professional or even taken on an iPhone. The main purpose of this photo is to draw people to click on your channel, so try and make it eye catching. A scientifically based trick is to include your face in the icon (if appropriate) and pull a face that's related to your YouTube channel (check out Vsauce's icon) or just a picture of you smiling.

 You can also use your channel name as inspiration for the logo. If you're really stuck, you can even go on the website fiverr.com and get a logo made for as little as $5, and they're very good quality. You can also get your pictures professionally edited to include your logo on them here. People also opt for drawn versions of themselves, and this can be really good, especially if you're not the most photogenic (like me).

You can also add a featured channels section, add a trailer to your channel, change how the videos are laid out and also enable 'channel comments' under the discussion section. Any change you desire to make can be done by clicking the settings icon (it is next to your subscribe button), then, enable the "customize the layout of your channel" option.

Channel Art

As mentioned previously, you can get a nice banner made for as low as $5 on fiverr, you can also use a free stock photo from pexels.com or use a wallpaper you like. This is not such an important part of your channel, you can perhaps use this to advertise a book you've released or have a link to your website on there.

Channel description

This part of your channel is important. Although the amount of people that check your channel description in relation to your subscribers is going to be fairly low, it's good to include links to any other social media profiles that you want to share and links to your website. Many YouTubers also include here a FAQ for questions you might be asked a lot. A crucial thing, if needed, is to include a business email here. Don't use your personal email. This can be extremely useful for increasing the revenue you make on YouTube, and we'll go into detail on this later in the book.

3. Start uploading your videos

Whenever you want to access the upload page, just log in and click the 'upload' button. Its position is at the top right-hand part of the YouTube website.

When you want to upload your videos, you can either...

- Drag videos to the upload page,
- Click the large upload area to browse for videos from your PC or
- Click the 'import' option, it is next to the 'import videos' area by the right of the upload page. This option allows you to upload videos you have saved in Google photos.

Another option that you can use is to make a photo slideshow for YouTube. It is available on the right-hand side of the upload page.

Pro tip: make sure you select either public, unlisted, private or scheduled as it suits you when you want to upload videos from your pc.

When you make your videos public, anyone can see it. When it is unlisted, only those that have the direct link can access the video. When it is private, only you can see it and you have to be logged in before you can see it.

When you want to schedule your videos, you can to set the time when it will be available to the public.

Other factors you need to keep in mind;

- If your web browser is up to date, the video you want to upload should have a maximum size of 128gb. Otherwise, you will only be able to upload a video with a maximum size of 20gb.

- Unless you verify your YouTube account, your videos cannot exceed 15 minutes in length. Once you have verified your YouTube account, this limit is removed.

- Make sure your videos are in mp4 format when you want to upload them. If not, you will get an "invalid file format" error. However, you can convert your video to an acceptable format.

- You can use YouTube's video editor to add titles, captions, split the video into clips, add photos and make video transitions.

- If you want to easily manage your videos, put them into custom playlists

CHAPTER 2

HOW TO MAKE GOOD CONTENT ON YOUTUBE

If you want to make good content on YouTube, here are 5 types of content you can create;

1. Comedy videos

Some of the most shared videos are comedy videos. They are often used to keep the audience pleasantly occupied.

It is a proven fact these types of channels have a higher number of subscribers than most network's comedy television shows.

Though the sense of humor is personal, there are a lot of comedy videos online and you can be sure you will find somebody who matches your style.

2. Unboxing videos

Though this might come as a surprise, it turns out that there are lots of people interested in watching someone else remove a new product from its packing.

This can also be product review videos.

It is a proven fact that most people would love to know other people's opinions about the products they want to buy before they actually buy it.

If it is positive, then, they make a purchase.

Hence, lots of people go on YouTube in search of reviews for the products they want to buy.

One major reason why YouTube has more advantage over other social media for this type of video is that you can display how you are using the product. For example, how you are applying the makeup, how you are test driving the car, how you are using the new kitchen gadget etc.

3. Video game walkthroughs

Here you will be playing a game. Then, you will make comment as you progress through the game.

One of the most popular video games is Minecraft. The major reason for its popularity is that the game can be modified with ease. Hence, you can use this feature in your videos and play as a modified character.

While there can be live play sessions, there can also be huge engagement between the gaming video makers and their supporters.

More about the equipment you might need to start making a gaming channel in upcoming chapters.

CHAPTER 3

HOW TO PICK A NICHE TO MAKE CONTENT ON AND MAKING CONTENT YOU'RE PASSIONATE ABOUT

Finding a niche can be extremely difficult when starting a channel. I struggled with the same thing when I started out with my channel; however, I discovered this 5-step trick that really helped me;

1. Find a piece of paper or something to write on.
2. Write down all of the niches you are considering.
3. List one and then number 1–10 underneath it

For example,

Niche: cooking

1.

2.

3.

4.

5.

6.

7.

8.

9.

10.

4. In the 10 blanks below each niche write down 10 video ideas.

For example; niche: cooking

- Best homemade sugar cookies tutorial
- How to properly frost a cake
- Chicken casserole tutorial

Till you reach number 10.

5. If you can't come up with 10 video ideas for a certain niche, that means it is too small of a niche and you should throw that idea away.

Those steps should have narrowed down your list of niches to only a couple really good ideas.

One simple and effective way to choose between the really good ideas is to pick the one that would be of interest to you on a long-term basis.

For example; assuming your two options are singing covers and cooking videos.

Now, imagine yourself 10 years from now.

Would you still be interested in making singing covers?

Would you still be interested in cooking videos 10 years from now?

If you still can't decide, put your two options in a hat, close your eyes and pick one.

CHAPTER 4

HOW TO GROW YOUR YOUTUBE CHANNEL AND MAKE MORE MONEY

You have to get serious about promoting your YouTube channel if you want to grow it and make more money.

In this chapter, you will discover my top 10 strategies and principles you can use to make YouTube's algorithm work in your favor.

Thus, you can grow your YouTube channel and make more money in the process.

1. Create custom thumbnails

Regardless of the quality of your video, if no one clicks on it, it is useless.

It is a proven fact that titles and thumbnails are two main factors people take into consideration before deciding to watch a video from a channel where they are not subscribers.

The thumbnail serves as a preview of your video especially when another user wants to embed your video on his site.

When you choose the custom thumbnail option, you can upload a video thumbnail immediately after uploading a video.

Also, you can add a custom thumbnail to an already existing video.

If you want to do this, here are the 3 steps you need to follow;

- Go to your 'video manager'
- Choose the video you want to work on and select 'edit'
- Select 'custom thumbnail'

When you want to create a killer title for your video, make it descriptive enough for someone to be interested. But it shouldn't be so long that it would be cut off when displayed.

Though you should include keywords to make it appear in search results and also include very attractive adjectives, don't make it so "over the top" that it seems spammy.

2. Increase your channel's watch time

One simple and effective way to do this is to get to the point quickly in your video; don't make your introduction too long.

Since the total watch time your videos accumulate is the most important metric here, you should ensure that you put more high-quality content in each video and not just fluff.

3. Emulate your previous top performing videos

Since you can determine your top performing videos, through your google analytics, you can figure out what these videos have in common and what promotional methods you used, then, repeat for future videos.

4. Add powerful 'call to actions'

This helps you to create engagement.

Your best option for doing this is through annotations.

If you have ever experienced annotations popping up right, left and center, then, you will know they can be really annoying.

Hence, don't destroy your user experience with hundreds of annotations.

Thus, use one annotation and make sure it is a form of call-to-action. For example, asking viewers to subscribe to your channel.

5. Promote your videos on other social media platforms

This is arguably the most effective way to grow your YouTube audience.

When you promote your videos on other social media platforms, you get...

- More views on your videos
- More people visiting your channel and becoming a subscriber

I strongly recommend that you promote your videos on Facebook, LinkedIn, Twitter and probably Google+.

Pro tip: create a mini promo Facebook video and link it to your YouTube video or your YouTube channel. The reason is that Facebook prefers users to make use of their Facebook live feature instead of sharing a YouTube link.

In addition, you can...

- Pin your videos to your Pinterest boards
- Blog about your latest video
- Add your videos to your presentations in SlideShare
- Scoop your videos on scoop.it and also suggest your videos to relevant topics on sccop.it

CHAPTER 5

HOW TO COLLABORATE WITH OTHER YOUTUBERS TO PROMOTE YOUR CHANNEL

When you want to get more subscribers to your YouTube channel, use collaborations. In the past, YouTube descriptions were used for this purpose, but now, there is a YouTube collaborator feature. When you use this feature, you can give credit to your collaborator by entering...

- His/her exact YouTube username
- His/her channel's URL

Here's a simple 3-step checklist you can use to the right collaborator for you;

1. **Compatibility**: This involves dealing with the potential collaborator's character or personality.
2. **Ideas**: If you are one initiating the partnership and you don't have an idea, there is no way you can get a collaboration
3. **Offer**: In most cases, collaborations involve one person who is more famous collaborating with another who is less famous than him. Hence, if you are the initiator of the collaboration, you need to discuss the kinds of offer you want to promote and how you will share the proceeds from the offer.

I highly recommend that you make these plans before contacting your potential collaborator. It will prove to him that you are serious about making it happen.

If you want to take full advantage of a YouTube collaboration to grow your channel, you need to promote the collaboration. You need to start planning on how to use social media to promote your video even before the video is released.

After the video is released, I recommend you start your promotion with the use of hashtags. When you use hashtags, you can start a conversation about your video and link them all together. Since most of the big brands are using hashtags to promote their videos, why shouldn't you?

For example, Heineken's hashtag is "#openyourworld".

If you want to encourage your fans to use your hashtags, put them right in the title.

In addition, you can...

- Write about the hashtag in your description
- Mention it in the video
- Use the hashtag as a YouTube card.

Your main goal is to ensure that your fans and your collaborator's fans are talking about this hashtag on social media; this will encourage more people to view the videos.

Hence, more social connections can now exist between the two fan bases.

-How To Find YouTubers Who Are Interested In Collaboration
Since most YouTube stars are always 'busy', you will have to look for other viable options especially if this is your first time of forming a collaboration.

Here are my top 7 places where you can find collaborators;

- Let's play collaboration thread on Reddit

- YTtalk forum
- The YouTube community forum
- DamnLag
- tube buddy community
- YTgamers forum
- YouTube partners on Google+

Pro tip: you will have a better chance of building a relationship with a potential collaborator if you spend more time getting yourself known on these forums.

CHAPTER 6: EQUIPMENT YOU MIGHT NEED TO START VLOGGING

In this chapter, you will discover the most important pieces of equipment you might need to start Vlogging.

Since your budget might be different from another person's budget, I will be giving the different options you can use to get started.

I have divided this into 3;

- Vlogging equipment if you are on a small budget
- Vlogging equipment if you on a 'medium' budget
- Vlogging equipment if you have a big budget

Let's get started with...

1. Vlogging equipment if you are on a small budget

If you are on a small budget, you can get started with your smartphone.

Though this will have an inferior sound and video quality compared to a camera and a mic.

You can use Microsoft movie maker to edit your videos, it is free.

Though it should come already installed on your pc; but if it doesn't, search for it on Microsoft play store or through google.

2. Vlogging equipment if you on a 'medium' budget

Here is the equipment you can buy if you have some cash to spend on equipment;

For the camera, I would suggest the Canon Powershot ELPH 110 HS 16.1MP CMOS digital camera. It will enable you to record your videos on 1080p HD. Obviously, this will improve the quality of the videos you will be putting out.

For the mic, I suggest the Manono lavalier microphone. You can clip it on your shirt; hence, the quality of your audio will be higher compared with the audio of the camera.

Both these are available on Amazon.

A more effective alternative to Manono lavalier microphone is a desktop mic. However, I suggest you only use this if most of your Vlogging will be done at home.

For the software, I suggest you continue using Microsoft moviemaker.

But if you feel limited by it, a more advanced option is Corel video studio pro X10.

If most of your Vlogging will be done while you are on the move, you will need to purchase a tripod stand.

One major benefit of the tripod stand is that you can extend the distance of the camera as you deem fit compared to using a camera which you cannot extend beyond the length of your arm.

Hence, it makes it possible for you to record yourself at different angles.

A very effective and durable tripod stand is the Ikross compact tripod stand mount holder. It is also available on Amazon.

Whether or not you need a lighting will depend on the place where you record.

But if you need a lighting, I recommend the Neewer 160 LED CN-160 dimmable digital camera/camcorder video light.

3. Vlogging equipment if you have a big budget

Though you have a big budget, it doesn't mean you should spend it lavishly to buy fancy equipment you may not know how to operate.

Hence, you can make use of the...

- Canon Powershot C7x Mark 11 digital camera as your camera
- Rode VideoMicro compact on-camera as your microphone
- Cyberlink PowerDirector 16 ultimate as your video editor
- Tripod stand mentioned above - Ikross compact tripod stand mount holder
- Aura ring light for your lighting especially for videos you will be shooting from your home. For videos you will be shooting outside your home, you can still make use of the one mentioned above - Neewer 160 LED CN-160 dimmable digital camera/camcorder video light.

CHAPTER 7

EQUIPMENT YOU MIGHT NEED TO START MAKING A GAMING CHANNEL

You have a choice whether to play video games for passion or as a hobby. There are YouTube stars who play video games, post it online and earn thousands if not millions of dollars in the process. Would you love to wake up, head over to your desk, play video games, then, get paid for doing so? If you answered yes to the above question, then, this is the most important report you will ever read.

Here are the 5 most important pieces of equipment you will ever need;

Important Equipment #1: A Recording Program

Obviously, you would need a recording program to record your gameplay before you can have a video.

Pro tip: choose any recording program that can record in HD. This will allow you to create a high-quality video.

Here are the 4 recording programs you will need;

1. **Nvidia shadowplay**

This software is not only free, but you can also download it on your computer.

If you want to capture screenshot up to 4k and stream games up to 1080p, Nvidia shadowplay is your best option.

The 4k screenshot is highly useful for YouTube thumbnails.

2. **Open broadcast software (OBS)**

In terms of functions, this is similar to Nvidia Shadowplay.

However, OBS is more effective for lots of live streaming than Nvidia Shadowplay.

3. Headset or microphone

Obviously, you need to record your voice when you record your videos.

As you must have known, a silent video is always very boring.

Your 2 best options for a microphone are:

- A headset which has a microphone you can connect to your PC
- A standalone microphone which you can prop on your desk. An example of this is the blue snowball ice microphone. If you are just getting started, I strongly recommend it to you since it has a decent sound quality.

Though you can make use of any headset you already own, the quality won't be as good as the snowball ice microphone.

Important Equipment #2: Editing Software

After recording your video, it is time to edit it. Editing is important because you might want to remove some parts completely, speed up some or add some Face-cam to your videos.

Put simply, when you make use of an editing program, you will create a video that is devoid of any abrupt interruptions. The best editing software that I recommend is the Sony Vegas movie studio platinum.

This software has an editing mode for making small changes. You can also make use of an advanced option to make as many changes as you'd like.

If you want to add overlays for reaction videos, this software is one of your best options.

You can start using it for free since it comes with a 30-day free trial.

Important Equipment #3: Camera

If you plan to do live reactions or you are okay with viewers seeing your face, then, a camera is important.

However, I strongly recommend that you use a webcam that can record 720p or higher. If the recording is lower than 720p, the quality of your videos will be very bad.

When you are starting your gaming channel, I recommend the Microsoft LifeCam H1.3000. I am recommending this for 2 main reasons;

- It is super affordable
- It streams at 720p

Important Equipment #4: Thumbnail Creator

The images you see before you play a video are known as thumbnails. The goal of an effective thumbnail is to attract viewers to your videos.

You can use either paid or free software to create a very attractive thumbnail. Photoshop is a very efficient paid option you can use to create your thumbnails.

However, if you are looking for a free alternative, then, gimp is your best option.

CHAPTER 8

HOW TO GET NOTICED ON YOUTUBE

Since YouTube can seem really crowded, in this chapter, you will discover my best tip on how you can get noticed plus the number one biggest mistake that I see people making on YouTube.

The number one way to get noticed is clarity. You want clear branding, clear messaging and especially clear content that's on a brand. Your uploaded videos and your interviews should all build on the same brand; focus is power. If you lack clarity, then you'll create confusion on YouTube. The biggest mistake that I see people making on YouTube is they're being too general and their messaging is unclear; focus is power. In addition, if you want to get noticed, here's a simple 10-step rule you should always follow;

- Build a community around your channel
- Make sure your videos are well scripted
- Plan to upload your videos at specific times of the week and maintain that period
- Optimize your videos - use annotations, tags, and a proper description of each your videos
- Use answerthepublic.com to create your keywords and video titles
- Don't forget to collaborate with other YouTubers. Re-read the chapter where we discussed collaborations.

If you spend the time to make quality videos, make your message right and continue to fine-tune your content, you will surely reap outstanding rewards.

CHAPTER 9

HOW YOUTUBERS MAKE MONEY

Below you will discover an estimated monthly income of 7 popular and perhaps, 'not so popular' YouTubers;

Name of YouTube channel	Estimated Monthly earnings
Pewdiepie	Over $1 million
Rooster teeth company	Over $1 million
Nigahiga	Over $240,000
Epic meal time	Over $250,000
Ruby rube $10,000	$10,000
Safiya Nygaard	$9,000
Wish shopping	Over $3,000

Most of these famous YouTubers make money in 2 major ways;

- YouTube AdSense
- Product placements and sponsorships

- **YouTube AdSense**

This can also be called built-in YouTube monetization.

In this model, you will earn a small fee when an ad is shown on your YouTube video and a viewer clicks on it.

Though it is very easy to make money this way, bear in mind that you need to have more than 10,000 total views before you can be admitted to the partner program.

How YouTube calculates your AdSense earnings?
Roughly, you'll get $7.50 for every 1,000 impressions. The impression is determined by the number of those who clicked and watched your ads.

Obviously, you won't be paid if the viewer either skips the ads, use an ad blocker or both. Hence, you may not earn much even if your video has lots of views. For example, if your video has 10,000 views but gathered only 3,000 impressions, you will earn just $22.50.

The key to maximizing revenues from this type of model is to determine the ads that work best for your audience.

For example, if your video is 3 minutes in length, then a pop-up ad will be more effective than a 30-seconds clip - all other things being equal.

- **Product placements and sponsorships**

This can also be called brand deals.

Funkee bunch (another famous YouTuber) have gone on to have over 4 million views on their video when they advertised the mobile phone game called friends.

Most times companies approach these famous YouTubers to make videos about their products or services in exchange for a flat fee or a commission based on the number of sales.

Pro tip: make sure you give a notification on your YouTube channel when you do a sponsored video.

Though most YouTubers make the majority of their earnings through these two ways, there are other ways you can earn on YouTube. These other ways will be discussed in the next chapter.

CHAPTER 10

HOW YOU CAN USE YOUTUBE TO MAKE MONEY

Obviously, you want to become a YouTube star and at the same time making hundreds of thousands of dollars per month or year in the process.

But the real question is... Is it that easy?

I will be brutally honest with you. The answer is No; it is not that easy.

In this chapter, you will discover 3 other major models of using YouTube to make money.

Let's jump right in...

Model 1: Affiliate Marketing
In this model, you will a percentage of the sales made when your viewers buy any product you recommend. This percentage is known as a commission.

If you want to improve your affiliate earnings,

- Pick a product suitable for your audience
- Create a video review of this product
- Put a link to buy the product in the description

Model 2: Sponsored Videos
You should only consider this option if your channel is popular.

In this model, you get sponsors who will pay you to display their product or services either at the beginning, the middle or the end of your video.

Model 3: Patreon
In this model, you will accept donations from your loyal fans in support of your creativity.

n exchange, you can give them some exclusive benefits for doing so. You can

get started by creating an account with Patreon on patreon.com

CONCLUSION

You just learned how to grow your YouTube channel and make money doing that. And that means you can now become a YouTuber who also makes money each month. To that end, let's quickly recap what you learned in the last 10 chapters:

You learned...

- How to make a YouTube channel
- How to make good content on YouTube
- How to pick a niche to make content on and making content you're passionate about
- How to grow your YouTube channel and make more money
- How to collaborate with other YouTubers to promote your channel
- Equipment you might need to start Vlogging
- Equipment you might need to start making a gaming channel
- How to get noticed on YouTube
- How YouTubers make money
- How you can use YouTube to make money

If you haven't already done so, go ahead and start taking action on what you have learnt. Then give yourself a pat on the back, because you're now all set to grow your YouTube channel and make money with it!

34123098R10021

Printed in Great Britain
by Amazon